T0171691

FROM **EDGINESS** TO **EAGERNESS**

─── *taking the Church back to willing service!* ───

TOBE MOMAH

FOREWORD BY DR. TIM TODD

WestBow
PRESS
A DIVISION OF THOMAS NELSON

ISBN: 978-1-4497-6215-5 (sc)
ISBN: 978-1-4497-6216-2 (e)

Library of Congress Control Number: 2012914372

WestBow Press books may be ordered through booksellers or by contacting:

WestBow Press
A Division of Thomas Nelson
1663 Liberty Drive
Bloomington, IN 47403
www.westbowpress.com
1-(866) 928-1240

Printed in the United States of America

WestBow Press rev. date: 8/20/2012

Table of Contents

Foreword

The person who is successful at being eager according to the Word of God is the one who will do what the average person will not do: submit wholeheartedly to God. Thinking wrong, believing wrong, and talking wrong always lead to an unhappy, mediocre, and unprofitable way of life and will cause you to be edgy.

To be enthusiastic for God, to become better, to believe big, and to strive to be above average in your eagerness to faithfully serve God, you must be willing to die to yourself and develop the right kind of mental processes.

You may think you have been programmed to be edgy, to be negative, disbelieve, to be skeptical. However, you can change. Those negative experiences—the minuses—can be transformed into positives and pluses simply by denying yourself, taking up your cross, and following Him.

Psychologist William James said, "The greatest discovery of my generation is that men can change their circumstances by changing their attitude of mind." We are taught that changing the input can change those thoughts. What goes in must come out. You can control your future, because you have the power to control your thoughts.

Philippians 2:5–8 says, "Let this mind be in you, which was also in Christ Jesus: Who, being in the form of God, thought it not robbery to be equal with God: But made himself of no reputation, and took upon him the form of a servant, and was made in the likeness of men: And being found in fashion as a man, he humbled himself, and became obedient unto death, even the death of the cross."

Some say success is just a decision anyway. That is true on the surface. But that decision must be backed up with solid effort. An eager person with a winning attitude accounts for 80 percent of the results in this country today. It's amazing that the figures don't change from year to year. They stay about the same. Twenty percent of the people are getting 80 percent of the results, and 80 percent of the people are getting 20 percent of the results. That isn't very much when you realize these figures haven't changed in the last twenty-five years.

Your growth potential, return on your investment, rewards in proportion to your efforts, and personal independence are limited only by your vision and desire. This already has made you above average. So be eager for God! You have a lot to be enthusiastic about. God created you in the likeness of Himself and endowed you with specific talents and abilities. As you develop those areas in your life and use them to help others, you won't have to be concerned about being above average. You will have conquered that enemy.

Dr. Tim Todd
President
Revival Fires International
www.RevivalFires.com
Proverbs 11:30

Preface

We live in the jet-set, instant generation that wants everything yesterday and nothing tomorrow. It is an age predicted by the prophet Nahum as edgy. Nahum 2:4 says a time will come when people shall, "rage in the streets [and] jostle one against another in the broad ways [for] they seem like torches and run like lightning."

That day is today; in the midst of worldwide financial upheaval and economic turmoil, God is calling us to rest and spiritual soliloquy with Him. Jesus was, like us, tempted in every way humanly possible (Hebrews 4:15) but came out unscathed.

Just as Jesus saw the "travail of His soul and was satisfied" (Isaiah 53:11), we also must pass through travails, not edgy, but eager to do His will. I am a witness to this paradigm shift, and my personal experience is highlighted in this book.

Our Lord Jesus Christ was eager to establish the kingdom of God on earth. In Luke 12:49, He says, "I am come to send fire on the earth and what will I, if it be already kindled?" Nobody associated with Jesus could be tepid or lukewarm. He says in Revelation 3:15–16, "thou art neither cold nor hot: I would thou wert cold or hot [but] because thou art lukewarm, and neither cold nor hot, I will spue thee out of my mouth."

Too many have brokered between cold and lukewarm for too long. The only church Jesus will rapture is not a cold or lukewarm church but a "glorious church, not having spot, or wrinkle, or any such thing [that is] holy and without blemish" (Ephesians 5:27). It is not a church of compromise but one of passionate conviction that He will come for. This book highlights the road to that passionate conviction and how the church can go from edginess to eagerness.

Tobe Momah

Acknowledgments

This book was born out of a desire to see a passionate church! It—the message—was planted in my heart while working at the Louisiana State Penitentiary Angola RE Barrow Treatment Center. I would like to thank Warden Burl Cain for using his office to give "lifers" and death-row inmates a life of passion through Christ in spite of their notable challenges.

The inspired stories I heard every day from prisoners whose lives have been changed by Christ made me realize how ineffective and dispassionate our churches have become from practicing mere religion. I would also like to thank Mrs. Burke, an astounding eighty-four-year-old retired teacher, who went beyond and above the call of duty to help edit this book. Without her, there would still be multiple errors in the manuscript and maybe no book published at all.

My wife of nine years, and the love of my life, endured long nights and endless weekends without me while I wrote this book. She gave her full cooperation and even called my noncommittal stand to correction when I failed to achieve deadlines or aspire to perfection in my writing. To her love, passion, and endless search for adventure and challenges I remain grateful. They formed a sounding board for a lot of material used in this book.

My pastor, Shane Warren, captured this book's essence in his sermons and gave me a future filled with expectancy. He showed me the power of relationships and stirred our church to see ourselves as high net worth caliber assets and not just church folk! Evangelist Tim Todd, who wrote my foreword, and the other pastors in the city of Monroe, Louisiana, also stand out for their scrupulous support and encouraging thoughts.

My family, including Dad and Mom, Dr Sam and Mrs. Momah,

and my brothers and sisters—Emeka, Nkem, Ada, Amaka and their spouses and children—stood shoulder to shoulder with me while writing this book. They never failed to provide support anytime I needed it (which was often), and for that, I am eternally grateful.

Finally, I would like to acknowledge my publisher, WestBow Press, for its awe-inspiring work and dedication to this book. My prayer is that God blesses all involved in this project, and as they made it happen for me, God will make it happen in their lives, too, in Jesus' name.

SIN WILL TAKE YOU FARTHER THAN YOU WANT TO GO, KEEP YOU LONGER THAN YOU WANT TO STAY, AND COST YOU MORE THAN YOU WANT TO PAY.

=PART I=

CHAPTER 1

Taking the Edge Off Our Razor-Thin World

[A]nd Jesus said to the disciples, come apart and rest a while for there were many coming and going and they had no leisure so much as to eat.   (Mark 6:31)

The people who follow God are called to peace not pieces (see Psalm 85:8); our existence should not be fraught with deadlines, pressures, and ultimatums but with freedom and rest. The prophet Isaiah says in Isaiah 30:15, "in returning and rest shall you be saved and in quietness and confidence shall be your strength."

To the contrary, our world today is dominated by deadlines justified by a means-to-an-end mentality. In pursuit of the proverbial Golden Fleece, there is an increase in rural to urban migration, where people live in inconducive environments and work in squalor just to accommodate their basic needs, such as education and health.

Unfortunately, the church has been infiltrated by this same *busy bug,* and instead of "waiting on the Lord," as prescribed in Isaiah 40:31, we are, for the most part, willy-nilly in our quest for the things of this world. The principle of "waiting upon the Lord [to] renew your strength and mount up with wings like Eagles" (Isaiah 40:31) is losing its appeal among today's instant generation and needs reawakening.

Modern Marvels or Urban Jungles?

In 2012, about half the world's population, 3.5 billion, lived in urban regions of the world, with 81 percent of them projected to be in the developing world by 2030. This has led to the twenty-first century being referred to in developmental circles as the "tipping point millennium."

With all these rural-to-urban migrations, facilities and social amenities in modern cities are overstretched. As a result, an increasing number of slums exist side by side with shiny skyscrapers in modern cities such as Mumbai, Nairobi, and Shanghai.

The People's Republic of China, for example, has more than 1 billion people in its urban areas, and 300 million more people are expected to move from rural areas to cities between 2009 and 2020. In Africa, 750 million, or more than 80 percent of the continent's population, are expected to live in cities by 2020. In India, 700 million more people will leave their rural villages for cities between 2001 and 2050, further exacerbating the already dense urban areas of India.

These accelerated migrations are caused by a desire for financial sustenance, health innovations, and social or academic pursuits. This pursuit for upward change is despite the lack of suitable accommodations or stable employment in the urban areas and causes more edginess in our modern world.

Busy or Blessed?

Mary and Martha were ardent supporters of Jesus' ministry; when Jesus passed through Judea, He called at their home regularly. While He was there, Martha criticized Mary's nonchalant attitude to household chores (Luke 10:40), asking Jesus, "Does thou not care that my sister has left me to serve alone?"

Martha, not stopping for a moment to hear the Master's instructions but nonetheless working for Him, represents the busy church today. She was busy but not blessed, a worker but not a worshipper. Jesus said that Mary had "chosen that good part [and] it shall not be taken away from her" (Luke 10:42).

Mary sat at Jesus' feet to hear the word, while Martha "was cumbered about with much serving" (Luke 10:40). That word "cumbered" means to drag around excess weight or be distracted. The lack of eagerness in Martha's world was a result of excess baggage from emotional, financial, and other multifaceted avenues.

To her, Jesus said, "You are careful and troubled about many things, but one thing is needful" (Luke 10:41–42). The way to leaving edginess and entering eagerness is by coming to Jesus, like Mary did, with those troubles and cares. Matthew 11:28 says, "Come unto me, all you that labor and are heavy laden and I will give you rest." First Peter 5:7 also asks us to "Cast all your cares upon Him; for He cares for you."

Too many of us are sucked into or distracted by our environment instead of focusing on the will of God. We fail not for lack of vision but for multiple visions and a lack of tenacity in accomplishing His will for our life.

Isaiah 42:3–4 tells us Jesus "will not break a bruised reed and a smoking flax He will not quench [but rather] bring forth judgment unto truth and not fail or be discouraged till He has set judgment on the earth." The eager stay focused, while the edgy fail from a plethora of causes that lack focus.

The Worried Well

At the turn of the twenty-first century, mood disorders (comprised of generalized anxiety disorder and depression) were called the "common cold" of medicine because of their increased prevalence, by 25 percent, among the US population.

A new category of patients has recently come to the fore: the "worried well." They are healthy, but their doctor's clean bill of health does not reassure them. They demand multiple scans and laboratory tests, attempting to identify what they don't have. They make up more than 25 percent of visits to physicians annually, causing a huge strain on medical resources for the community.

The reason for this surge in the worried well is the information glut available through the media. The average adult spends twenty eight to thirty hours watching television per week. This impairs Bible learning, stunts relationships and exacerbates fears.

The Lost Art of Leisure

When Jesus saw that the disciples were on edge with not even time to eat, He suggested that they "come apart and rest a while" (Mark 6:31). He wanted them to have some leisure time away from the hustle and bustle of the crowds and, therefore, put them on His boat for a time of private introspection.

The church needs to rediscover the lost art of leisure in a lost and dying world on the edge. It was after they were refreshed that they were able to minister to five thousand men with two fish and five loaves (see Mark 6:36–42).

The Bible says in 1 John 5:3b, "His commandments are not grievous." When obeying God becomes a burden rather than a delight, you have moved from eagerness to edginess. You need to rediscover the art of leisure by resting in Him.

HEAVEN DOESN'T HELP THOSE HELPING THEMSELVES BUT THOSE WHO THROW THEIR LIVES INTO JESUS' EVERLASTING ARMS.

CHAPTER 2

Everlasting Arms

The Eternal God is thy refuge and underneath are the everlasting arms; and He shall thrust out the enemy from before thee and shall say, destroy them.

(Deuteronomy 33:27)

O ur world is a dangerous world. Women are gang raped every thirty seconds, precious saints are martyred every five minutes, and an unborn baby is killed by abortion every twenty seconds.

In Psalm 74:11–20, the psalmist prays for God to "withdraw his right hand out of His bosom ... because the dark places of the earth are full of the habitations of cruelty."

The only secure place in our depraved and nasty world is in His everlasting arms. When we are in His arms, we can be sure "no evil shall befall us and no plague come near our dwelling" (Psalm 91:10).

The Path of the Eagle

When God brought the children of Israel out of Egypt, He "bare them on eagles' wings and brought them unto Himself" (Exodus 19:4). What we need as Christians in our pluralistic, agnostic, and postmodern Christian culture is to ride high on the wings of the Spirit, away from secular and worldly influences.

In Isaiah 33:16, the prophet says that He who dwells with the everlasting burnings, "will dwell on high, his place of defense shall be the munitions of rocks, bread shall be given him and his water are sure." One of the attributes of an eagle is its keenness of vision. The eagle has the ability to see five times as far as a human with perfect vision and can spot an animal the size of a rabbit two miles away.

When God says we "mount up with wings like eagles" (Isaiah 40:31), it attests to what our vision can see from afar. There is "a path that no fowl knows and which the vulture's eye has not seen" (Job 28:7), but is clear to the eagle. As we fly on eagle wings, we see what natural man cannot see—the path of the eagle. That path is where rest is guaranteed.

The Way to God's Pleasure

Everything we do is for His pleasure. Revelation 4:11 says, "God has created all things and for His pleasure they are and were created." We are created to bring Him pleasure, but we do that only when we submit our will to His!

Philippians 2:13 says, "For it is God which works in you both to will and to do of His good pleasure." Before God can do in you what He masterly created you for, He must shape your will. Until you are willing, you can't be obedient; until you are obedient, you can't bring Him good pleasure.

Isaiah 1:19–20 says, "If you are willing and obedient, you shall eat the good of the land but if you refuse and rebel, you shall be devoured by the sword." The way to God's pleasure is a willing submission to His will. Until we submit, we can never fulfill our life purpose but will remain victims of life.

=PART II=

WILLING SERVICE

- **WILLING SERVICE**
  The Example of Jesus

- **WILLING SERVICE**
  Paul's Eager Liberty

- **WILLING SERVICE**
  The Mistake of Peter

IF YOU WERE ARRESTED
FOR BEING A CHRISTIAN,
WOULD THERE BE
ENOUGH EVIDENCE
TO CONVICT YOU?

CHAPTER 3

Willing Service:
The Example of Jesus

It pleased the Lord to bruise Him and put Him to grief.
When you make His soul an offering for sin, He shall see His
seed and be satisfied for He shall bear their iniquities.

(Isaiah 53:10–11)

Nobody epitomizes the heart of a willing servant as does Jesus; He served the disciples (see Luke 22:27) without ego or pride and died on the cross for the whole world, "yet He opened not His mouth but as a sheep before the shearers is dumb, so he opened not His mouth" (Isaiah 53:7).

He submitted willingly to the death of the cross. John 10:18 says that He "laid it down of Himself [for] He had power to lay it down and power to take it up again." It was that willingness that made "the pleasure of the Lord to prosper in His hands" (Isaiah 53:10b).

He told His Father, "I delight to do thy will, O my God [and] come in the volume of the book as it is written of me" (Psalm 40:7–8). He embraced His commission and went to the cross willingly for us, and by doing so, "raised many sons unto glory" (Hebrews 2:10).

Meat from Mean Men

Many of us have no problem submitting our will to the pleasure of good men but would withdraw when it involves submitting to haters and backbiters. Those with whom we don't often get along are, however, those we win with our willingness to serve in spite of past misgivings.

In John 4:34, Jesus told His disciples, "My meat is to do the will of Him that sent me and to finish His work." This involved dying on the cross, being spat on, the ripping of his back with shears, and receiving every disease known to man on His body. Yet He willingly offered up Himself!

Jesus was eager to offer up Himself because He likened the experience of dying to one of a satisfying meal, even if it were for the benefit of mean men. John 4:32, 34 says, "He said unto them, I have meat to eat that ye know not of ... My meat is to do the will of him that sent me and to finish his work."

We are called to serve with eagerness, even though not all we serve will be worthy of our service. According to Ephesians 6:7, we must serve "as servants of Christ (by) doing the will of God from the heart and with good will doing service, as to the Lord and not to men."

Rest Assured

When Jesus invited His disciples to "Come unto me, all you that labor and are heavy laden and I will give you rest" (Matthew 11:28), He was offering them a rest that was assured. It was not based on the economy, politics, or societal norms but on surrendering to the will of the Father.

Jesus was not an edgy leader; He prepared His disciples for His departure and advocated peace even in the midst of swords. He, "knowing all things that should come upon Him" (John 18:4), surrendered to the soldiers before they even attempted to arrest Him.

Jesus always knew what to do before an occasion presented itself. For example, in the feeding of the five thousand in John 6:5–6, Jesus asked Phillip, "Where shall we buy bread that these may eat? And this He said to test him for He (already) knew what He would do." A leader best leads from an assured place (with eagerness) and not on the edge, as so many of our risk-minded franchises advocate.

**PASSION +
VISION +
COMMISSION =
FULFILLMENT**

CHAPTER 4

Willing Service:
Paul's Eager Liberty

*All they asked was that we should continue to remember
the poor, the very thing I had been eager to do all along.*
(Galatians 2:10)

Paul came to Christ burning with eager liberty. Before his
conversion, Paul had been "kicking against the pricks" (Acts
4:10), a condition referred to as offering vain and perilous resistance
to God. After his conversion, Paul turned that edginess into eagerness
in his service for Christ.

In Acts 21:13b he says, "I am ready not only to be bound but also to
die at Jerusalem for the name of our Lord Jesus." He was willing not just
to live for Christ but also, if need be, to die for Him. That is eagerness!

He told the disciples that He was always "eager to remember the poor"
(Galatians 2:10), not out of compulsion, but by choice. That word "eager"
means passionate, to do speedily or with urgency, and we, as Christians,
have to be passionate to effectively communicate the good news.

The Reward of Willing Service

The apostle Paul, a man God used to reach his world, says in
1 Corinthians 9:17, "for if I do this thing (i.e., preach the gospel)
willingly I will have a reward but if against my will, a dispensation of
the gospel is committed unto me."

He would receive a reward only if preached willingly! Anything else would make his service economical but not rewarding. The word used for dispensation in 1 Corinthians 9:17 means to economize or manage. When our work isn't willing service, we are managers not makers and collectors instead of creators of reward.

In Deuteronomy 28:47–48, God told the Israelites, "Because you served not the Lord with joyfulness and gladness of heart for the abundance of all things ... you shall serve your enemies in hunger and want for all things." How willing your service to God is will determine what you will want for in life!

Living with Passion

Paul lived his life with passion. He told the people of Athens, "For in Him (God) I live, move and have my being" (Acts 17:28). God is a passionate, not a passive, God. In John 2:17, Jesus says, "The zeal of (God's) house hath eaten Me up."

He warned the Church of Laodecia that because "they were neither hot or cold (but) lukewarm, He (Jesus) would spue them out of His mouth" (Revelation 3:15, 16). Jesus portrayed the last-day church in His letter to the seven churches and, like the Laodecian Church, today's churches have lost passion for God and live life passively. Such people will not stay in God's presence.

Living with passion epitomizes the eager liberty Paul pursued. In 2 Corinthians 12:14, 15, he told the church in Corinth that "he seeks not theirs but them and will very gladly spend and be spent for them though the more abundantly he loves them, the less he be loved." He added in Romans 10:1, "my heart's desire and prayer to God for Israel is that they may be saved."

Eager liberty does not want to enslave others but to empower them. Paul pursued the gospel of liberty even when it was at variance with the leadership of the church in Jerusalem. In Galatians 2:11–13, he singled out Peter and Barnabas for acting hypocritically in the presence of Jews to put unnecessary burdens on the gentile Christians.

He preached an open-faced gospel—one devoid of middlemen or apparitions—where in the presence of the Spirit of God there was liberty (2 Corinthians 3:17–18). This eagerness was in contrast to the veiled-face gospel (2 Corinthian 3:13–16), which represents uncertainty or edginess.

THERE CAN BE NO
SUITABLE USE OF
YOUR SKILL WITHOUT
THE SUBMISSION
OF YOUR WILL.

CHAPTER 5

Willing Service:
The Mistake of Peter

*Peter said, not so Lord for I have never eaten anything that
is common or unclean and the voice said, what God has
cleansed call not uncommon.* (Acts 10:14)

Peter was called, I believe in Acts 10:14–16, to take the gospel
to the uncircumcised but because he was unwilling to change
his stereotypical thinking about Gentiles, he eventually became the
apostle to the circumcised only (see Galatians 2:7).

Many of us have lost opportunities because we were unwilling or,
like Peter, who "doubted in himself what the vision he had seen should
mean" (Acts 10:17), been unnecessarily legalistic or liturgical.

The man who doubts is likened to him "that wavers ... (for) let
not that man think he shall receive any thing from the Lord" (James
1:6, 7). The mistake of Peter was doubt; he called the Gentiles what
God didn't and lived only on the edge of his potential.

Peter Knew Better!

Peter had seen Jesus heal, save, and deliver from the "gutter-most"
to the uttermost. He knew Jesus had come to "save that which was
lost" (Matthew 18:11) and had commissioned them to take the "gospel
to the ends of the earth" (Acts 1:8). Yet he hesitated when it involved
the Gentiles.

In Galatians 2:11–14, Paul challenged Peter's hypocritical living.

Peter claimed he was comfortable with Gentiles in the absence of the Jewish leadership of the Church, but in their presence, he separated himself from them. He was eager to take the gospel to the Jews but edgy when taking the gospel to the Gentiles.

In Acts 11:17, when asked to explain how the Gentiles received the gift of the Holy Spirit, Peter says, "Forasmuch as God gave them the like gift as he did unto us, who believed on the Lord Jesus, what was I, that I could withstand God?"

He stood aloof as God baptized the Gentiles in Cornelius's home (see Acts 10:44–45). Rather than go along completely with God, Peter, like several Christians today, lived without conviction and passion. They watch things happen rather than make them happen!

Eagerless Excuses!

Moses, like Peter, was a leader mightily used in his generation but who failed to attain God's best. Even though he was God's agent in bringing Israel into its Promised Land, Moses made a plethora of excuses in Exodus 4:10, because he was not eager to undertake the task.

He eventually angered God by telling Him to "send someone else" (Exodus 4:13). He was almost killed by the Lord for not circumcising his first son (see Exodus 4:24–26) and was, like Peter, doing God's will against his will.

The man who makes excuses has lost his eagerness or passion for God! For King Saul, making excuses became a favorite pastime, and it cost him the throne. In 1 Samuel 13:12, he "forced himself and offered a burnt offering" rather than wait for Samuel. That excuse cost him the throne (1 Samuel 13:14).

Saul lost the kingship of Israel because he made countless excuses for inexcusable behavior and lacked godly passion. In 1 Samuel 28:17–18, Samuel says to Saul, "The Lord hath rent the kingdom out of thy hand and given it to thy neighbor because thou obeyed not the voice of the Lord nor executed His fierce wrath upon Amalek."

This porosity of passion sealed Saul's fate; it stemmed from a lack of eagerness and an excusing existence. When asked why he hadn't killed King Agag and the choice cattle of the Amalekites, Saul said, "The people took the spoil, which should have been utterly destroyed, to sacrifice unto the Lord" (1 Samuel 15:21). Excuses are the sign of a lack of eagerness and the hallmark of an edgy life.

=PART III=

FROM JELLY TO JEWEL

**THE SECRET TO LIFE
IS BEING FULL OF GOD
AND EMPTY OF SELF.**

CHAPTER 6

From Jelly to Jewel:
The Example of Gideon

Nobody epitomizes a transformation from edginess to eagerness as much as Gideon. He lived on the edge politically, religiously, and economically but was transformed from a jelly to a jewel by a divine encounter. In Judges 6, Gideon went from the least in his father's house and one who could not speak out against Baal, to a mighty man of valor.

When the angel of the Lord saw him initially, he was in his winepress, hiding to thresh wheat (Judges 6:11). But at the height of his reign, he dominated the Midianites for forty years and ruled over Israel in peace.

What took this insecure, scared, and frail boy to the pinnacle of an illustrious career as a deliverer in Israel is the secret to why some end up jewels and some end up as jelly.

What Changed in Gideon

Three things spurred a counterculture revolution in Gideon's soul: commission, camouflage, and conversation. He went from being a young man afraid of pulling down his father's idols in Judges 7:27 to attacking a million Amalekites and Midianites with only three hundred men.

He went from being edgy about attacking the enemy to being eager and fully persuaded about the project. His eagerness triggered the immediate mobilization of his 300-man army, and when their trumpets sounded in the camp of the Midianites and Amalekites, a fiasco occurred that resulted in Gideon's triumph.

Like Gideon, some of us have failed in the past—economically, religiously, and politically. The greatest failure, however, is not the man who fails but the man who for fear of failing does nothing. Your best times are ahead of you if you, like Gideon, apply His commission, camouflage, and conversation to your everyday Christian walk.

The Lost Mrs. Lot

Mrs. Lot was unsure about her husband's decision to leave Sodom and Gomorrah. She enjoyed her friends and the company she hung around with in Sodom and Gomorrah. She would miss their gossiping, comparison of trends, and never-ceasing, irreligious behaviors (2 Peter 2:7, 8).

She and her husband were edgy about leaving Sodom and "while they lingered, the angel of God laid hold upon their hands, the Lord being merciful unto them, and brought them forth saying escape for thy life and look not behind thee" (Genesis 19:16, 17).

Mrs. Lot, unfortunately, looked back and became a pillar of salt (Genesis 19:26); her halfhearted mission was over. Taking a lesson from what happened to her, the rest of her family escaped the consequences of a halfhearted response to God's word by escaping to the mountains and not the surrounding hills as previously provided (Genesis 19:19–21, 30).

She became jelly instead of the jewel God intended for her. This happened because of her edginess and refusal to let sin go totally. God does not call us to halfhearted service but to full commitment. He says in Colossians 3:23–24, "Whatsoever ye do, do it heartily, as to the Lord, and not unto men; Knowing that of the Lord Ye shall receive the reward of the inheritance."

Missing Your Mission!

The mission must be done wholeheartedly or not at all. When God told David that his son Solomon would build the great temple in Jerusalem for His name's sake, David asked Solomon to "serve God with a perfect heart and a willing mind for the Lord searches the hearts" (1 Chronicles 28:9a).

The difference between the service that makes one a jewel and the one that makes you jelly is willingness in your heart to obey and not the act of obedience itself. Isaiah 1:19 says, "If you are willing and obedient you will eat the good of the land," and Malachi 3:17 says, "in that day when God makes up His jewels, (He) will spare them as a man spares his own son that serves him."

Jesus told a parable about two sons in Matthew 21:28–32 who were asked by their father to work in his vineyard. The first son initially refused, then repented, and worked the vineyard; the second son, on the other hand, agreed to go and work but never did. Jesus likened the Jewish oligarchy of His day to the second son, because they promised but did not perform.

It is more than just service God seeks. He seeks those who will serve Him "in truth and spirit" (John 4:23) and not with words alone. God "sees not as man sees for man looks at the outward appearance but God looks on the heart" (1 Samuel 16:7).

WHOEVER PRECEDES YOU PREVENTS OR PROSPERS YOU.

CHAPTER 7

From Jelly to Jewel:
Commission

[A]nd the Lord said unto Gideon, by the three hundred men that lapped will I save you and deliver the Midianites into thine hand ... and the same night the Lord said unto him, arise, get thee down unto the host for I have delivered it into thine hand.
(Judges 7:7–9)

Without a commission, there can be no mission! God is committed only to those He calls and will save only those He sends. Gideon conquered the armies gathered against his makeshift force with eagerness, because He had heard the Word of God.

Too many have only vague, uncertain, and unclear visions or commissions. As a result, their lives become uncertain and unclear. This condition is contrary to God's will for us. Paul says in 1 Corinthians 9:26, "Therefore so run I not as uncertainly; so fight I, not as one that beats the air."

God commissioned Jeremiah as a prophet to the nations in Jeremiah 1:5. He asked Jeremiah, "What seeth thou?" in verse 11, to which Jeremiah replied, "I see a rod of an almond tree" (Jeremiah 1:11b). Because Jeremiah saw the vision clearly, God says, "I will hasten my word to perform it" (Jeremiah 1:12).

God is eager to commission us, but the commission must first be clear to us before we can make it clear to the world around us. The prophet Habakkuk said, "I will stand upon my watch ... to see what

God will say unto me" (Habakkuk 2:1). In the following verse, God told him, "Write the vision and make it plain." Until it is plain to you, you can't make it plain to anyone else.

The Power of a Godly Commission

Jesus could do no mighty works until He was commissioned by the Holy Ghost with power at the River Jordan (Mark 1:10; Acts 10:38). The early Church were asked by Jesus to "tarry in the city of Jerusalem until they be endued with power from on high" (Luke 24:49).

With a godly commission, you have the arsenal of heaven—including angels, anointing, and His Word—at your disposal. The Bible asks in 1 Corinthians 9:7, "Who goes to war anytime at his own charge and who plants a vineyard and eats not the fruit?" You are God's charge as long as you go at His charge, not man's.

David was commissioned king not by man but by God. When Samuel anointed him king in 1 Samuel 16:13, he used a horn filled with oil, and not a man-made vial (as in the case with King Saul), to signify divine commission. Paul, speaking about David, says, "He served his own generation by the will of God" (Acts 13:36). You will give more to your generation when you determine your commission, not before!

God, the Golden Guide

With God as your guide, you will be strong for the battle, never wrong, and always in front in life. The Bible says in Psalm 18:30, "God's way is perfect." It encourages us to "come boldly unto the throne of grace that we may obtain mercy, and find grace to help in time of need" (Hebrews 4:16).

Where God guides, He guards! Whoever walks or follows His paths prospers. In 2 Chronicles 31:21, it says King Hezekiah, "began in the service of the Lord (by) seeking God and doing it with all His heart and (so) prospered." Our attitude must be one of eagerness with the commission as the foundation.

The wise man in Proverbs 3:5 says, "Trust in the Lord with all thine heart and lean not unto thine own understanding. In all thy ways acknowledge Him and He shall direct thy path." He directs, but only when you deny your human reasoning and follow Him fully! James 1:5–6a says, "If any of you lack wisdom, let him ask of God, that gives to all men liberally and upbraideth not and it shall be given him but let him ask in faith, nothing wavering."

WHAT THE WORLD CALLS
DELUSION, GOD CALLS
DIVINE DISGUISE!

CHAPTER 8

From Jelly to Jewel:
Camouflage

*I (God) have delivered it (the Amalektes and Midianites)
into thine hand but if thou fear to go down, go with Phurah
thy servant down to the host.*   (Judges 7:9, 10)

In the book of Judges, Gideon went down to the host of the
Midianites and Amalekites with his servant Phurah because he
was afraid. The meaning of the name *Phurah* in Hebrew is ornament
or camouflage and demonstrates how fear is dispelled when we go out
in God's camouflage!

It was in Phurah's company that fearful and insecure Gideon
became bold and assertive. This is the same man who, when greeted by
the angel as "a mighty man of valor" (Judges 6:12–14), demurred and
called himself the least of the least (Judges 6:15). In Judges 8:18–19,
he describes himself as the King's child, because he began to see as
God sees.

When God wants to bless you, He sends someone into your life. In
the case of Gideon, that person was Phurah. He camouflaged Gideon's
secret fears with faith and strengthened his hands. Gideon, as a result,
won a great victory for Israel.

Facts Are Not Always True!

God called Abraham and Sarah "the father and mother of
multitudes" years before they had Isaac (see Genesis 17:5, 15). Rather

than rely on expert facts, Abraham and Sarah did the impossible by seeing the invisible. God "quickens the dead and calls those things that are not as though they were" (Romans 4:17).

It was a fact that they had passed the age of reproduction. It was a fact that Sarah's womb was dead. But because they were "fully persuaded that what He had promised, He was able also to perform" (Romans 4:21), they brought forth their promise.

In a world such as ours, we need to start speaking what God says by calling the things that are not as if they are. We must hold the promises of God higher than the facts of man. We must believe these promises so much that we see and speak of them as though they were already reality.

Fake It 'til You Make It!

It is not what you have but who you believe that determines your outcome. In the life and ministry of Jesus, He spoke to the potentials of people and not to their problems. For example, He told Jarius his dead daughter "was not dead but sleeping" (Mark 5:39). He asked the man born blind to walk two miles to the pool of Siloam with spittle on his eyes (John 9:7) if he wanted to be healed, and asked the man with the withered hand to stretch out the hand that was acknowledged as dead (Matthew 12:13).

All faked it before they made it. Jarius believed contrary to widespread opinion, and his daughter was raised from the dead (Mark 5:42). The blind man walked two miles to the pool of Siloam, washed, and came back able to see (John 9:11). And the man with the withered hand stretched it out and received an instant miracle of regeneration (Matthew 12:13).

Jesus told Thomas, "Because you have seen me you have believed. Blessed are they that have not seen, and yet believed" (John 20:29). The individuals who believe without the facts are the truly blessed ones. They stand in expectation and corroborate it with their actions. Blind Bartimaeus threw away garments that denoted him as a blind beggar the minute Jesus called him (Mark 10:50). Mordecai took off his sackcloth attire after interceding for Esther and the Jews (see Esther 4:1, 5:9), who were earmarked for elimination by King Ahasuerus, because he lived out what he believed.

Faith is only true when it goes against a fact. Hebrews 11:1 says, "Faith is the substance of things hoped for (and) the evidence of things not seen." If you can see it or feel it, you don't need faith! Faith acts on the invisible and believes in the impossible!

WHAT YOU SAY IS WHAT YOU SEE, AND WHAT YOU SEE IS WHO YOU BECOME.

CHAPTER 9

From Jelly to Jewel:
Conversation

Then they that feared the Lord spake often one to another and the Lord hearkened and a book of remembrance was written for them ... (so) they shall be His in that day when He makes up His Jewels. (Malachi 3:16, 17)

What you hear is what you think, and what you think is what you become. When Gideon was strategically placed to hear a conversation between two Midianite soldiers (Judges 7:15), his faith was stirred, and he attempted the impossible.

The conversation about a barley cake tumbling into the camp of the Midianites and squashing it (Judges 7:13, 14) strengthened Gideon's hands and saved Israel from defeat. One sentence took him from edginess to eagerness, and God can do this for you.

We can defeat our enemies by making godly conversation. Mark 11:23 says, "Whosoever shall say unto this mountain, be thou removed and be thou cast into the sea and shall not doubt in his heart, but shall believe that those things which he saith shall come to pass, he shall have whatsoever he says."

Not Calling a Confederacy

In Isaiah 8:11–12, the prophet Isaiah says, "For the Lord spake thus to me with a strong hand, and instructed me that I should not walk in the way of this people (by) saying a confederacy to all them to whom this people shall say, a confederacy, neither fear ye their fear nor be afraid."

The Hebrew word for confederacy means conspiracy or treason. The above Scripture adjures us not to repeat the mistakes of the world around us by speaking as the world speaks. We must speak as God's speaks.

While the Israelites were calling themselves grasshoppers in comparison to the Anakims and saying they were not able to take the land (Numbers 13:31–33), Joshua and Caleb "stilled the people saying let us go up at once and possess it; for we are well able to overcome it" (Numbers 13:30).

Those who brought the evil report died instantly (Numbers 14:37), while Caleb and Joshua, who spoke God's word, thrived for another forty plus years. Our edgy and brutish life stems from not speaking in faith.

Life and Death in the Tongue

In Proverbs 18:20–21, the wise man says, "A man's belly shall be satisfied with the fruit of his mouth; … (for) Death and life are in the power of the tongue: and they that love it shall eat the fruit thereof."

Until you start saying it, you won't see it! In Psalm 91:2, the psalmist says, "I will say of the Lord, He is my refuge and my fortress; my God in Him will I trust." Verses 9 and 10 of the same psalm reiterates this. They say, "Because I have made the Lord, which is my refuge, my habitation there shall no evil befall me and neither shall any plague come near my dwelling."

It was his saying so (verse 2) that caused the manifestation of God's presence and protection. It is not an occasional speaking but a continual speaking that brings results. Psalm 35:27–28 says, "Let them shout for joy, and be glad, that favor my righteous cause: yea, let them say continually let the Lord be magnified … And my tongue shall speak of thy righteousness and of thy praise all day long."

Let the Redeemed Say So

Most times, our enemy is our own mouth! Instead of saying who we are in Christ—that is, the redeemed—we speak of what the Devil has done. Psalm 107:2 says, "Let the redeemed of the Lord say so, whom God has redeemed from the hand of the enemy." If we don't say so, it won't be so.

Until the prophets Haggai and Zechariah prophesied God's Word to the Jewish settlers of Jerusalem (Ezra 5:1–2), the inhabitants were edgy—not eager—to finish the house of God they had started. Ezra 6:14 says, "The elders of the Jews built, and they prospered through the prophesying of Haggai and Zechariah (so that they) built and finished it according to the commandment of the Lord."

Your conversation determines your condition. As long as the Israelites listened to their enemies, they dilly-dallied, doddered, and became derelict. But when they spoke the Word of God to each other, they finished what they started. First Peter 3:10 says, "For he that will love life, and see good days, let him refrain his tongue from evil, and his lips that they speak no guile."

=PART IV=

- **EAGERNESS FOR EXPLOITS AND EXCELLENCE**

- **STUFFY SPIRITS**

- **MAKING THAT MOVE**

WHAT YOU ADMIRE YOU ATTRACT, AND WHAT YOU DESPISE, YOU DENY ENTRY IN YOUR LIFE.

CHAPTER 10

Eagerness for Exploits and Excellence

His people will be willing in the day of His power.
(Psalm 110:3)

Paul was passionate about excellence and performed exploits for the kingdom. It was, however, all related to his eagerness to win the lost! In Philippians 1:20, he says, "According to my earnest expectation and hope that in nothing I shall be ashamed, but that with all boldness magnify Christ in my body, whether it be by life, or by death."

That word "earnest" used in that passage also means "eagerness." In Colossians 3:23–24, Paul advises us, "and whatsoever you do, do it heartily, as to the Lord, and not unto men; knowing that of the Lord you shall receive the reward of the inheritance: for ye serve the Lord Christ."

Your inheritance in Christ is tied to your eagerness. If you do what you do passionately and consistently, without eye service, doors of inheritance will open to you. It is not an episodic earnestness God seeks but an eternal eagerness—whatever the weather, season, or gathering.

Eternal Excellency

You are not supposed to be earnest today and dour tomorrow; He wants you earnest eternally. Isaiah 60:15 says because, "thou hast been forsaken and hated, so that no man went through thee, I (God) will make you an *eternal excellency,* a joy of many generations."

Too many leave church on Sunday eager to take on the world. But when faced with Monday morning deadlines and swashbuckling bosses, they become less than eager. If behavior and attitude are not consistent, they will not yield fruit. Deuteronomy 22:9 says, "You shall not sow thy vineyard with divers seeds lest the fruit of thy seed which thou hast sown and the fruit of thy vineyard be defiled."

Deuteronomy 22:10 says, "You shall not plow with an ox and an ass together." An ox represents a hardworking and go-getting attitude, but an ass stands for stubborn, stupid, and sour attitudes in workers who use their circumstances as an excuse to underproduce.

A Mind to Work

Nothing great has ever been achieved by a mind that was not willing to be great! Solomon was attested by his progeny as "a great king of Israel (who) built and set up" (Ezra 5:11) God's temple. For him to have achieved such monumental work, he had to be, first and foremost, willing.

First Chronicles 28:9 says David advised Solomon to "serve Him with a perfect heart and with a willing mind for the Lord searcheth all hearts and understands all the imaginations of the thoughts." His willingness to be used by God—otherwise defined as eagerness—spiraled him to the top of his generation as the wealthiest and wisest man.

Nehemiah, speaking in Nehemiah 4:6 about the workers on the devastated walls of Jerusalem, says, "So we built the wall; and all the wall was joined together unto the half thereof: for the people had a mind to work." Regardless of the skills in a mind's repository, until it is submitted to God's will, that mind will be unfruitful because of unwillingness.

A Covenant of Peace for a Man of Passion

Phinehas attacked the Midianitish woman and her Israeli lover with a spear, and in the process, stemmed an already deadly plague (Numbers 25:7–9). His action, born out of eagerness, brought a perpetual covenant of peace on his progeny.

God says in Numbers 25:12–13, "I give unto him (Phinehas) my covenant of peace: And he shall have it, and his seed after him, even the covenant of an everlasting priesthood because he was zealous for his God, and made an atonement for the children of Israel."

The rest of the leadership were edgy or unsure what to do when Zimri brought Cozby into the tent of prayer, but Phinehas was eager and assertive. He obtained an unprecedented blessing from the Lord as a result of that. Your passion determines your peace, and the more extreme your eagerness, the more perpetual your peace.

Our Lord Jesus was a man of great passion, and it resulted in the triumph of His soul. Hebrews 1:9 says He, "loved righteousness and hated iniquity; therefore, God anointed Him with the oil of gladness above His fellows." Your passion or eagerness determines your peace and joy in life. Jesus loved—not just lived—righteousness. He hated—not just harried—iniquity and became the most important landmark for life.

GOD DOES NOT RESIDE WHERE HE DOES NOT REIGN!

CHAPTER 11

Stuffy Spirits

Restore unto me the joy of thy salvation and uphold me with thy free Spirit. Then will I teach transgressors thy ways and sinners shall be converted unto thee.

(Psalm 51:12, 13)

To be "free-spirited" is not always a connotation of liberal, ungodly thinking. In Psalm 51:12–13, it is described as the conduit pipe to fruitful living. Everything else is to be "stuffy spirited."

To be "stuffy-spirited" is to be regimented, obnoxious, and dogmatic in one's outlook toward God. In other words, it means staying edgy when God has called us to eagerness. It could mean laboring when God has called us to liberty.

In 2 Corinthians 3:17–18, the Bible says, "where the Spirit of the Lord is, there is liberty. (But) we all with open face beholding as in a glass the glory of God are changed into the same image from glory to glory."

Until you sow in liberty, you can't reap the incremental glory God wants for you. A sincere spirit, not a stuffy one, is what transforms someone. Paul tells us in Philippians 1:10–11 to "be sincere and without offence till the day of Christ (and so) be filled with the fruits of righteousness."

Borderline Believers

Obadiah 1:7 says, "All the men of thy (Esau's) confederacy have brought thee even to the border (so that) the men who were at peace with you have deceived you and prevailed against you, (and) they that eat thy bread have laid a wound under thee."

Borderline believers live on the edge and don't give up room for God to enlarge them. They often suffer betrayal and defeat because of their edginess. If they open up and let God enlarge the place of their feet, they can conquer and not be conquered. The psalmist says in Psalm 18:36, "God hast enlarged my steps under me that my feet did not slip."

Nobody knows what tomorrow holds except God (James 4:14–15). Because we know He alone holds tomorrow, we should step out with God in faith eagerly, because He enlarges borderline believers' feet to stand sure.

David's Delight versus Saul's Stuffiness

In a spiritually stuffy world, people like David are a breath of fresh air. He says to God in Psalm 40:8, "I delight to do thy will." In contrast, Saul saw doing God's will as a burden, not a delight. In 1 Samuel 15:21, he tersely replies to Samuel's inquisition about why the Amalekites were spared, "The people brought the spoil to sacrifice unto the Lord your God."

Saul saw God as Samuel's alter ego. He was stuffed up with so much personal insecurity, envy, and wrath that he saw God's assignment to wipe off the Amalekites as a burden and not as a delight. His rebellion contrasts with David's reveling in God! To David, it was not a burden to obey God but a delight!

The reason for a burdensome and edgy lifestyle is the lack of a personal relationship with the Father. Saul saw God as Samuel's God and not his personal Lord to be trusted and obeyed. Until we have a personal relationship with God in prayer and worship, we lose our rest in Him (Matthew 11:28) and remain on the edge.

COURAGE WITHOUT COMMUNION IS CALAMITY!

CHAPTER 12

Making That Move

The hour cometh, and now is, when the true worshippers shall worship the Father in spirit and in truth: for the Father seeketh such to worship him. (John 4:23)

Gideon made that move from edginess to eagerness and triumphed over the host of Midian (Judges 7:20–22). His triumph heralded the beginning of his leadership tree, as the people asked him to "rule over us, both you, your son and your son's son for you have delivered us from the hand of Midian" (Judges 8:22).

Our eagerness in serving God is not just for the here and now, but it determines where we spend eternity. First Timothy 6:17–19 says that those who are rich in this world should trust in God and not their riches. They should "be willing to communicate; (laying) in store for themselves a good foundation against the time to come, (and) lay hold on eternal life."

We must serve God willingly if we are to lay a good foundation for our eternal future. Our will can be a spiritual tool for eternal benefits or a demonic route to perdition. Hebrews 10:35 says, "Cast not away therefore your confidence, which hath great recompense of reward." How we use our will on earth can determine where we will be in eternity!

TEN KEYS TO NONEDGY, EAGER SERVICE!

1) **FULNESS OF LOVE:** Galatians 5:13b–14 says, "by love serve one another. For all the law is fulfilled in one word, even in this; thou shall love thy neighbor as thyself." Love is the only thing required to keep God's law, and without it, service becomes drudgery.

2) **FAITH:** Who you believe will determine the eagerness of your work for the Master! It says in 1 Timothy 6:17–18 that the rich should not "trust in uncertain riches, but in the living God ... that they be rich in good works, ready to distribute, willing to communicate." An attitude of faith not only stirs you to eager service but provokes those around you to do the same.

3) **FORGIVENESS:** Until you let go of hurts, anger, and bitterness, your service to God will not be perfect but replete with edgy repetition. King Amaziah "did that which was right in the sight of the Lord but not with a perfect heart" (2 Chronicles 25:2). His heart was not perfect, because he harbored an inner resentment for the men who had killed his father, King Joash (2 Chronicles 25:3). He eventually killed them a few years into his reign, but by then, bitterness had killed his life and ministry.

4) **FORGETTING:** Your willingness to forget will revolutionize your walk with and your work for God. In Philippians 3:13, Paul says, "One thing I do (is) forget those things which are behind and reach for those things which are before." The reaching for those things that are before connotes Paul's eagerness in service and would not have been possible without forgetting.

5) **FEAR GOD:** Until you fear God, you will always fear something or someone less than God. Until you are broken by God, you remain breakable in the hands of men. Psalm 51:16, 17 says, "For Thou desirest not sacrifice ... delightest not in burnt offering. The sacrifices of God are a broken spirit and a contrite heart, O God, Thou will not despise." He doesn't want your sacrifice but your surrender! Surrender is what brokenness and fearing God is all about.

6) **FUNDING FAITHFULLY:** In Matthew 19:20, Jesus tells the story of the rich young ruler who had obeyed the law from birth

but was unwilling to give away his riches and receive treasure in heaven by following Jesus. His unwillingness to give was born out of an edgy lifestyle that was noneager, stereotypical, and methodical. His response to Jesus in Matthew 19:20b—"all these things (the law) have I kept from my youth up: what lack I yet?"—shows an orthodox, legalistic mind-set. He was not an outlandishly in love follower of Jesus and sadly, "went away sorrowful" (Matthew 19:22), like so many edgy givers today. Second Corinthians 9:7b says, "God loves a cheerful giver."

7) **FUN-FILLED SERVICE:** Deuteronomy 28:47–48 says, "Because thou served not the Lord thy God with joyfulness and with gladness of heart, for the abundance of all things, they shall serve their enemies." Whom you serve is because of how you serve! If you serve in fun, you will not find anything lacking in your life.

8) **FOLLOWING THE WORD:** Jesus "humbled himself and became obedient unto death, unto the death, even the death of the cross" (Philippians 2:9a). God, therefore, highly exalted Him and gave Him a name above every other name so that at the mention of His name, every knee shall bow and every tongue confess Jesus as Lord (Philippians 2:9). His willingness to humble himself and die on the cross changed the course of history. Your humility toward God will make you willing to serve others.

9) **FLOCKING TOGETHER:** The church is only as strong as its members stay or flock together. In John 17:23 Jesus prays, "that they may be made perfect in one." Our unity heals, helps, and holds up our message and makes us eager to serve. In Zephaniah 3:9, God says, "I will turn to the people a pure language, that they may all call upon the name of the Lord to serve him with one consent." Before we begin serving, we must be in unity, speak the same language, and focus on Him in prayer.

10) **FLESH DESTRUCTION:** It is through destruction of the flesh that we can eagerly serve in the kingdom of God. Paul quotes Jesus in 2 Corinthians 12:9, "'My grace is sufficient for thee: for My strength is made perfect in weakness.'" The weakness of

his flesh made the power and grace of God available. That same grace is available to us today. Romans 5:17 says, "If by one man's offence death reigned by one; much more they which receive abundance of grace and of the gift of righteousness shall reign in life by one, Jesus Christ."